Credit Score

How to Remove all Negative Items from Your Credit Report and Boost Your Credit Score by 100 Points in 30 Days or Less

By Mark Bresett

© Copyright 2017 by Mark Bresett - All rights reserved.

The follow book is reproduced below with the goal of providing information that is as accurate and reliable as possible. Regardless, purchasing this book can be seen as consent to the fact that both the publisher and the author of this book are in no way experts on the topics discussed within and that any recommendations or suggestions that are made herein are for entertainment purposes only. Professionals should be consulted as needed prior to undertaking any of the action endorsed herein.

This declaration is deemed fair and valid by both the American Bar Association and the Committee of Publishers Association and is legally binding throughout the United States.

Furthermore, the transmission, duplication or reproduction of any of the following work including specific information will be considered an illegal act irrespective of if it is done electronically or in print. This extends to creating a secondary or tertiary copy of the work or a recorded copy and is only allowed with express written consent from the Publisher. All additional right reserved.

The information in the following pages is broadly considered to be a truthful and accurate account of facts and as such any inattention, use or misuse of the information in question by the reader will render any resulting actions solely under their purview. There are no scenarios in which the publisher or the original author of this work can be in any fashion deemed liable for any hardship or damages that may befall them after undertaking information described herein.

Additionally, the information in the following pages is intended only for informational purposes and should thus be thought of as universal. As befitting its nature, it is presented without assurance regarding its prolonged validity or interim quality. Trademarks that are mentioned are done without written consent and can in no way be considered an endorsement from the trademark holder.

Table of Contents

Introduction 1

Chapter 1: What Your Credit Score is and What It Means 3

Chapter 2: How to Obtain a Free Credit Report 15

Chapter 3: Curbing Debt 23

Chapter 4: Credit Mistakes 31

Chapter 5: Credit Boosting 39

Conclusion 45

Introduction

Thank you for purchasing *Credit Score: How to Remove all Negative Items from Your Credit Report and Boost Your Credit Score by 100 Points in 30 Days or Less and congratulations on taking the first step towards having an improved credit score.* Whether it is a desire to build credit for the first time, fix bad credit, or to turn an okay credit score into a great one, there is no denying that good credit is extremely important. Credit can be seen as valuable, if not more so, than a person's actual net worth and having a good line of credit can open many doors that may be closed otherwise.

The following chapters will discuss the process to significantly boost your credit score in a short amount of time. Everything ranging from what the difference between a credit score and a credit report is, to how to fix common mistakes on your credit report that are not your fault, will be explained. No detail is overlooked, and that is so that you are armed with all of the tools and knowledge necessary to meet your goal of improving your credit score.

Simply spending less and saving more is often considered the de facto method of improving a credit score, but this book will show you that there are far more efficient and easy ways to quickly bring that score up to a more satisfying number. None of the information within this book is daunting and you will see how it really is possible to gain 100 points in a month or less.

Credit Score

There are plenty of books on improving your credit score, so thank you once more choosing this one. Every effort was made in the writing of this book to ensure it is full of as much useful and practical information as possible. Please, enjoy!

Chapter 1
What Your Credit Score is and What It Means

A person's credit score is perhaps the most important financial asset to have. It is used as a determining factor in many things ranging from qualifying for a loan to landing a job. In the United States, a credit score can be seen as more important and more valuable that an individual's net worth. Banks, lenders, financial institutions, and government institutions all use a person's a credit score to figure out if somebody is going to be a liability or hindrance should the institution decide to do business with the individual. When it comes to credit there is simply no way to overstate how important it is.

So, what exactly is a credit score? A credit score is a number that is generated based on the analysis of a person's credit files and that represents how much creditworthiness they have. This number is gathered from credit bureaus which have created credit reports for this specific purpose. In order to create these credit reports the credit bureaus take a look at various factors and assign them values based on how much of a risk a person is to the bureau. As an example, FICO, one of the larger credit institutions, disclosed a general make up of exactly what is factored into a credit score. It should be noted that a FICO score is not the same as a credit score but rather a FICO score is a type of credit score.

A credit score is generally composed of 10% type of credit used, 10% credit search, 15% age of credit history, 30% debt accumulation, and 35% payment history. The precise formula for a credit score is not known to the public as a rule. The components just shown are a generalization and the percentages vary with each credit institution.

This leads to a very important thing to remember when it comes to credit: there is more than one credit score since each bureau has their own credit score. The idea that there is only one universal credit score is just a product of misinformation. There are three major credit bureaus that are responsible for compiling the credit information into credit reports that are then used for credit scores. These bureaus are Equifax, Experian, and TransUnion.

Each of the bureaus has grown to become established credit institutions in not just the United States, but around the world. Because of their wide reach the information they provide is invaluable. Lenders, consumers, employers, and all manner of financial institutions use the information that the three major bureaus supply. It is with this understanding that each of the bureaus will be looked at in detail.

The first to be discussed is TransUnion. TransUnion provides information in over 30 countries to roughly 45,000 business and 500 million consumers. These numbers are not only impressive but also make it the 3rd largest credit bureau in the United States. TransUnion formed in 1968 under the parent company of Union

Tank Car Company and served the role of a holding company for the larger organization. In 1969, it became the owner of the Credit Bureau of Cook County and became responsible for maintaining almost 4 million card files. Later in 1981 the Marmon Group purchased TransUnion for $688 million. Goldman Sachs Capital Partners later purchased it in 2010. Four years after that TransUnion bought the data company TLO and in 2015 it became a publicly traded company. The years of acquiring companies and becoming acquired resulted in TransUnion becoming a business that offers predictive data that determines a consumer's ability to repay loans study debt behavior.

Experian is the second of the three big bureaus used for credit scoring. It is a global company that operates in 40 countries with the corporate headquarters located in Dublin, Ireland. Formerly known as TRW Information Services, it became the bureau that it is today through a series of business deals dating back to the 1970s. GUS plc, a retail company located in the UK, allowed for the then novel idea of letting customers purchase products on credit. A computer programmer that worked for the company named John Peace combined all of the mail order data that the various branches of GUS utilized in order to create a central database. The database was later expanded with electoral roll data and was commercialized in 1980 under the new name of Commercial Credit Nottingham (CCN). It was then in 1996 that GUS plc purchased Experian and merged it into the CCN. This is when Experian began to broaden its range and enter new markets around the globe before separating from GUS in 2006 to once again be its own independent entity, only now it had greater resources and capital that would lead to it becoming one of the three major bureaus.

The last of the major bureaus is Equifax. Of the three it is the oldest, having first been founded as far back as 1899. It covers information for over 88 million businesses and more than 800 million consumers. Equifax was originally founded as Retail Credit Company based out of Atlanta, GA and rapidly grew as a company. By 1920 the company had spread throughout not just the United States but also Canada. Just a few decades later it had already grown to become one of the largest credit bureaus in America with files held on millions of citizens in North America.

The majority of Retail Credit Company's business came from creating reports for insurance companies when customers would apply for new policies. RCC was so efficient at this that the company became the main reporters for all of the major insurance companies.

The information that was investigated included more than just an individual's finances or health, but also a person's habits, morals, and other such statistics. This created controversy for the company during the 1960s and 1970s due to not just the information collected but also the company's willingness to sell the information to virtually anyone. Some of the more controversial information collected included a person's marital troubles, school history, political activities, and even their sex life.

Because of this the US Congress had to hold a hearing when RCC attempted to computerize its records. The hearings led to the Fair Credit Reporting Act which regulated information stored about consumers by corporations. In an effort to improve the damage caused to their company image RCC changed their name to Equifax in 1975. Under the new name the company phased out insurance reporting and focused more on credit reporting.

Together these three bureaus are the primary sources of credit reports for credit scores. Each bureau supplies its own credit report and credit score that can go on to make up an individual's entire credit history. They are not the only sources of credit services, however, as there is a financial institution that is often used in conjunction with the big three bureaus that is known is FICO.

FICO is a data analytics company focused on credit scoring. It was created in 1956 by Bill Fair and Earl Isaac. The pair met when they were both working at the Stanford Research Institute in California. The company went through a number of name changes over the years. Originally it was called Fair, Isaac and Company after the name sake of the two founders. It was then changed to Fair Isaac Corporation in 2003 before finally taking the abbreviation of FICO as the official name in 2009.

While the FICO score is the most utilized score, it is not the only score available. All credit scores that are not derived from FICO are referred to as educational credit scores. An example of an education score is VantageScore. VantageScore is a relatively newer score among the credit-reporting agencies. It was created in 2006 by the three major bureaus in an attempt to compete against FICO. It is jointly owned by Equifax, Experian, and TransUnion yet it is maintained and manages as an independent company called VantageScore Solutions, LLC.

Much like FICO, VantageScore's credit scoring models uses data collected by the three major bureaus to predict the risk a potential consumer would pose and the to determine how likely they are to default on a loan. Also like FICO, VantageScore utilizes a three-digit scoring system which uses higher scores to indicate lower risks. Despite the surface level similarities between FICO and VantageScore there are some differences.

The most obvious difference is that VantageScore's design model makes it possible to be operational with all of the three bureaus' data, as opposed to FICO which has a different model for each. What this means for the consumer is that rather than having to receive credit reports and credit scores from each of the bureaus as they would with FICO, they simply require only one report and one score from VantageScore. Another difference is that how VantageScore calculates its scores. While FICO gives generalized percentages detailing how it comes to a credit score, VantageScore does not give any percentages. Instead of a number indicating the weight a credit item carries the calculations are created thusly: payment history is indicated as being extremely influential, the type and age of credit as well as the percentage of a credit limit that is used are weighted as highly influential, total debt/balance is moderately influential, lastly both recent credit and available credit are weighted as less influential.

CE Score is another different score and is published by CE Analytics. It is used by such sites as Community Empower and iQualifier.com. While it is free for consumers to obtain the score, it is distributed to 6,500 lenders throughout the Credit Plus network.

Given the amount of information that is gathered in a credit report it is important to know just how that information is used. A person's credit has an effect on several major financial activities that they would want to pursue. Some of the activities are obvious, others may be surprising.

Perhaps the most well-known affect a person's credit has is the ability to get a loan from the bank. If a person has good credit then the bank is more likely to do business with them as the credit report is an indicator of the person's ability to pay back the loan. This means that anybody looking for a loan for a home, car, or new business would have an easier time getting the bank to cooperate with them and give them a loan. On top of being more likely to receive the loan, a person with a good credit score can also expect to have a much more manageable interest rate. The bank trusts the person to make payments on time and does not expect the person to be much of a risk. The person is seen as dependable so the bank is not going to apply any pressure to ensure they are paid back.

Another obvious effect is how a person's ability to get a credit card is affected. The same rules for getting a loan from a bank apply to getting a credit card with a few differences. A person with a less than perfect credit score can still get a credit card, but there will be some restrictions in place. A person may be only to get a credit card from specific companies and with a much smaller spending limit, for example. The interest rate may also be much higher because the individual is seen as a greater risk.

The ability to rent or purchase a home is also based on a person's credit. Landlords look at a person's credit to determine if they are not only trustworthy but if they are dependable enough to pay rent on time consistently. The interest rate on a person's mortgage depends on the credit of the individual. The lower the score then the worst the interest is for the person.

Utilities are also affected by a person's credit. The utilities companies may charge extra fees or higher rates to a person with less than perfect credit. With the higher fees attached to utilities ultimately a person may have higher bills month to month. This means that instead of having a normal power bill, for example, the individual has to incur a greater fee that they otherwise would not have to pay if their credit was in a better standing. Cellphone providers and insurance agencies may also do the same as the utilities, with the former having the ability to not just restrict the level of service a customer may receive but even outright turn down customers.

What Your Credit Score is and What It Means

One of the more surprising impacts of a person's credit is on their romantic relationships. Studies have shown that those with good credit tend to have stronger relationships that last longer. An interesting fact that should be taken into consideration is that those of similar credit standings often end up having successful relationships as well. This is because similar credit standings, whether good or bad, can be seen as an indicator about their attitude towards money and finances. Simply put, those who have similar attitudes towards money are more likely to be compatible in other areas as well. However, it should not be ignored that 40% of adults are stated, according to these studies, as saying that knowing a person's credit score affects their desire to date that person.

This is due to the fact that when a couple is applying for a loan together, both of their credit reports are taken into consideration. If one person has great credit but the other doesn't then the lower credit score could prevent the couple from receiving the loan. This creates a feeling of being a burden on the person that has the lower credit score and can lead to hostilities.

The fact of the matter is that a good credit from one person in the couple does not cancel out the bad credit of the other person. Credit simply does not work in a way that would allow that to be case. Instead the bad credit weighs both individuals down and causes the person with good standing in their credit to incur the same penalties as the other, especially if they filed jointly for any financial endeavor. For example, if the couple were to apply for a home loan together the good credit of the one individual would not boost the standing of the other's bad credit. This is because negative and positive items in credit reports are weighted differently from each other. As stated earlier a person's debt accounts for approximately 30% of their credit score according to FICO while something positive such as the age of a credit line accounts for only 15%. The numbers simply do not add up and this leaves the couple in a bad position to get a loan. This and other financial issues can, and often do, lead to huge strains on a couple that results in an unfortunately poor relationship.

One last major impact of a person's credit score is also a controversial one. A person's ability to get a job is often affected by their credit. While there is little direct correlation between a person's job performance and their credit history, employers still use a credit check to screen potential employees. The reasoning behind this is that employers are attempting to reduce liabilities such as theft potential and want to assess how trustworthy an employee would be if hired in to the company. Due to the lack of correlation between job performance and credit, a small number of states (including Connecticut and Illinois) have either banned or heavily restricted the practice of using a credit score to screen employees. Not every employer utilizes credit screening, but the employers most likely to do so are financial institutions and federal jobs due to the sensitive nature of their work. It should be noted that Eric Rosenberg of TransUnion who is the director of relations with state government has stated on record that no research at all shows any statistical correlation between a person's job performance, their likelihood to commit fraud against their employer, and the individual's credit report.

Taken in broader strokes the use of credit scores for anything other than determining the financial risk factor has been met with criticism. Even the case for using a credit score to analyze a person's financial risk has been called outdated and controversial. Due to this, Golden West Financial, the company that merged with Wachovia Bank, actually abandoned FICO scores all together. Instead of relying on FICO scores they adopted a type of analysis that, while being costlier, is able to look at a potential client's employment history and assets before offering them a loan.

The last of the criticisms is that many may be inaccurately labeled as being untrustworthy and of greater risk than they actually are. What this means is that a person who by all means is financially secure may be assessed as having a lower credit score because they either self finance their expenses or because they do not have multiple credit cards. People like this would have to drastically change their financial situation in order to grow positive credit despite the fact that by any other measurement they are financially secure and not a risk.

Despite the criticisms and controversies regarding credit scores, there is simply no denying the importance credit has in a person's financial status and their ability to lead a productive life.

The FICO scores, credit scores, and credit reports all serve the purpose of indicating how much a risk or liability an individual could possibly be to a given institution. Lenders and banks use these scores to determine if a person is able to get a loan or not. Employers use these scores to assess the likelihood a potential employee is going to commit any sort of fraud against them. And even personal relationships are made or broken based on the credit standing of the individuals involved. There is a very good reason why people often say that credit is more important than wealth, and these examples of just how far reaching of an effect credit can have. So, of course, the best course of action an individual can begin to take is to understand their credit as thoroughly as possible.

Chapter 2
How to Obtain a Free Credit Report

The first step towards any sort of progress is to learn where you stand. This is true for education, relationships, and even a new exercise regimen. This is also true for improving a person's credit. Before a person can begin to boost their credit score they must first learn where they stand. Knowing this information lets the person know what steps they have to make next in order to get the score they desire.

To learn this information a person has to obtain a credit report. A credit report is not the same thing as a credit score or a FICO score. It is a record of a person's relevant credit history that has data collected from a variety of sources such as banks, lenders, and federal institutions. The credit score is the end result of the algorithm that has been applied to the credit report to act as a predictor of delinquent financial risks and behaviors. An analogy that may help understand the difference is that a credit report like is a report card from grade school while the credit score is if all of the grades on the report card were averaged out to one grade. It is not a perfect analogy but it may help in understanding the difference.

How a credit report is created is a process that involved multiple sets of data and it all begins with a person doing something as seemingly innocuous as applying for credit. When a person does apply for credit with any institution that information is then sent to one of the major credit bureaus such as Equifax or TransUnion. The bureau takes that information and matches it with identifying information that is kept on record such as the individuals name or address. Once the match is made lenders use the gathered records to figure out just what a person's risk factor and credit worthiness are. The individual's ability (or inability) to repay debts is determined by the amount tracking if past payments have been made on time and consistently. This information is what makes up a person's credit report and having this information goes a long way towards building proper credit and improving their score.

Getting a free credit report is the necessary first step towards building a better credit score. Obtaining a credit report is the legal right of every United States resident. It didn't always used to be so, but the Fair and Accurate Credit Transactions Act (FACT Act) of 2003 allowed consumers to receive a free credit report once a year from each of the big three bureaus. Also under the Wall Street Reform bill of 2010, a consumer is able to obtain a free credit score if they have been turned down for a loan or insurance as a result of their credit.

There are several places a person can receive their free credit report online. These services often provide more than just a credit report. Some offer tools to help a person plan for the future and try to predict how financial actions they are planning could change their credit score. Some also feature credit monitoring that allow users to stay up to date on any changes to their credit. When it comes to getting a free credit report there is no wrong or bad place to request a report from as the information is always useful and legally accurate. However, there are a few online resources that stand out from the rest in the level of service and features they provide a person who not only wants to obtain a free credit report but also wants to utilize a host of tools.

One of the more popular services is Credit Karma. The global finance company was founded in 2007 by Ryan Graciano, Nichole Mustard, and Kenneth Lin. It was created with the goal of giving consumers quick and easy access to their credit scores after Kenneth Lin became frustrated trying to find his own credit score. He saw the opportunity in offering others the ability to receive their own credit scores and decided to partner with Graciano and Mustard to create Credit Karma.

Credit Karma offers a number of services to consumers, all of which are free. First of all, it provides free credit scores and free credit reports from the TransUnion and Equifax bureaus. It does not receive a credit report or score from Equifax to provide to the consumers, unfortunately. Credit Karma provides daily credit monitoring and even gives consumers weekly updates on their credit scores and credit reports.

In addition to this Credit Karma has a number of other tools available for use. For example, Credit Karma has a service that allows a person to find any money that could be owed to them legally. Perhaps a person missed a check and has not realized it. This tool would show the individual that they have unclaimed money available in their name. Credit Karma also has resources for personal loans and auto insurance. Based on the user's credit score and credit report, Credit Karma matches a person with a loan or insurance that would be a great fit for them. Along the same lines credit cards are also suggested to users based on their credit. This can be useful for those who are worried about being unable to obtain a credit card due to their credit. They can be shown that anybody is able to get a credit card that fits their needs. Financial calculators are also available to simulate future credit scores, calculate debt repayment time frames, and even estimate loan payments plus interest rates.

Credit Karma provides tools for any financial situation, all for free. On top of the services the website offers it also has a large number of community options and discussions that serve to give advice on a variety of financial subjects ranging from Credit Karma itself to saving for retirement.

The resources the website has are invaluable to consumers due to not just being able to get a free credit report and free credit score, but for also being able to use the wide variety of services that all serve to help a person improve their finances.

Another popular website for consumers is Credit Sesame. Initially conceived in 2010, the company was founded by Adrian Nazari who had also been a founder of Financial Crossing, Inc. and chairman of the board at Financial Circuit, Inc.

Credit Sesame receives the information for the free credit reports from TransUnion only, which should not be seen as a negative. Receiving a free credit report from any of the big three bureaus' data is a huge benefit to the consumer. What makes Credit Sesame different is that it is focused not only on the free credit reports and free credit scores, but also on loans. As of early 2016 Credit Sesame's registered users had over $100 billion in loans combined across 8 million accounts. That is an impressive feat for such a young company.

Like Credit Karma, Credit Sesame also has free credit monitoring for registered users. This allows people to be able to track their credit score and credit report for changes. The changes may not come from financial actions of the consumer, however, but could be caused by identity theft. Protection from such actions as identity theft is also offered for free by Credit Sesame. Credit Karma also offers identity theft protection, yet Credit Sesame has a stronger emphasis of it as a service. This is likely due to the fact that it does not offer the same variety of services so it makes up for it by having stronger services.

The last of the popular websites to explore is the aptly named Credit.com. This website is perhaps the most informative of those discussed in this book. It has the financial advice for a wide swath of topics in detail ranging from credit repair to understanding what the worst mistakes are when it comes to buying a car. The usefulness of this sort of information cannot be overstated and serves to highlight the difference between Credit.com and other popular websites.

Like other websites Credit.com offers free credit scores and free credit reports. The source of the information used is from Experian, meaning that Equifax and TransUnion do not factor into the credit information. Also, similar to the other websites is the fact that Credit.com allows the consumer to look for loans and credit cards based on their personal financial situation.

There are far more resources available when it comes to obtaining a free credit report and free credit score, however the ones discussed here are among the most popular and useful. They offer more robust options than many other competitive websites and provide tools that serve the greater purpose of giving a person greater control over their credit. Annualcreditreport.com is an example of such a website that offers free credit reports and free credit scores. What makes it different is that the three major bureaus have jointly created it in cooperation with the FTC.

It should not be ignored the level of impact having access to a free credit report and a free credit score can have. Knowledge and access to information of this level allows for an individual to begin taking huge steps to improving their credit score. Given the fact that the information is free is little reason to ignore the opportunity of obtaining a credit report and credit score. It would be next to impossible to improve a person's credit standing without having this level of access and it is almost worrying to consider that it is only in recent years that the public has been able to learn this information about their own credit. Because of the newfound ability to access this information many people have begun to take matters into their own hands when it comes to improving their credit and learning how to work within the system to their benefits. Perhaps most importantly is that people are learning how to manage their assets and also their debts.

Chapter 3
Curbing Debt

When it comes to credit, finances, and improving one's credit status there is one giant elephant in the room and it is called debt. Student loan debt, credit card debt, loans, mortgages, medical bills, and many more are all debts that people will incur over a life time. Unsurprisingly these debts can have negative impacts on a person's credit should they go unpaid. If that does happen, for any given reason, then there are a number of ways to reduce debt and even begin to improve a person's credit score.

The first thing to do is also the easiest of all. It is simple enough that many already do it without realizing how important it can be when it comes to paying down debt. This first step is merely creating a budget. This should be no surprise but a budget is a simple way to show yourself exactly what is available to spend, how much should be saved, and what needs to be paid. There are many who rely on memorizing this information or they just pay bills as they come, but these methods lead to people often spending money they don't have, then when a bill shows up they are unable to pay on time. A budget allows for proper planning and should be utilized without question, and just like getting a credit score and a credit report knowing what one has to work with makes every following step much easier.

Budgeting is often considered an activity that requires a person to be overly analytical and borderline neurotic. The public image is often one of an individual incessantly clipping coupons and going to extreme lengths just to save $1. While these activities are useful, for those that wish to go to these lengths then especially so, they are not exactly necessary. Creating a budget does not have to mean eating the cheapest and smallest amount of tasteless food for dinner, nor does it mean having to sift through newspapers and magazines with a pair of scissors in order to find the coupons that offer the best deals. Creating a budget is simply just the act of creating a visible system knowing how to spend one's money.

A working budget is a type of budget that is designed not to pinch pennies but to act as a display for the individual of where their money should be going. Limiting one's spending does help, yes, but if a person is living a comfortable and affordable life then there may not necessarily be a reason to change this. The working budget displays factors such as what bills are due and when so that there are no surprises in store down the line. It also displays what is available to be spent on what luxury, such as having $20 saved away for a movie ticket at the end of a week. This is all a working budget is, just a display of what an individual has.

The benefits of having this working budget is that in addition knowing what is due and when, it eliminates the guessing game of what an individual has to spend. In other words, it is keeping tabs on their money much like a credit report.

In addition to creating a working budget an important idea to remember is to pay more than is due on a credit card, if possible.

The reasoning behind this is a very simple one, the sooner that debt is paid off then the better it is in the long run. Paying more than the minimum amount on a credit card means that the interest rate is not going to be as painful over time. A person does not have to worry about a 10% interest rate over just as many years if they paid off the credit card in 2 years instead.

In order to get the additional means to pay off the credit card debt could mean living below one's means. Doing so is generally considered good advice regardless of one's financial state or goal. It is a great way to save money and reduce financial risk. A person living below their means is more likely to have money saved for a medical emergency than somebody who lives more exorbitantly.

This may seem contrary to what was stated earlier with regards to creating a working budget but there is a difference between living below one's means and living frugally. There is nothing wrong with an occasional luxury so long as it is budgeted for and the individual is able to make up for the spending quickly. Living below one's means is about reducing excessive spending and unnecessary purchases. However, for some this actually could mean living as frugal and thrifty a life as possible and if such is the case then there is nothing against that action at all. There are those who find such a lifestyle quite liberating as once they get their finances on a better track they realize that the more expensive items they used to adorn their lives where not needed and that they could be happier and more productive without those luxuries.

Another way to reduce credit card debt is to take advantage of balance transfers. If a person possesses a credit card with a high interest rate but they are able to pay it off in a few months, then it may be wise to actually transfer the balance to another card that has a zero-interest balance transfer. This method of consolidation can save money and reduce debt that one would normally incur at the same time. This is sometimes called a snowball effect, as the high interest rate is being rolled "downhill" to a lower one.

Transferring the balance of high interest card to a zero-interest balance card is a time-tested method of reducing debt. Instead of paying the higher interest a person could instead be paying a much smaller payment without incurring any sort of negative impact on their account. This is an ingenious idea that will come up again and again in this book as it should definitely be taken to heart. There simply is no simpler way to put it, but this method is a fantastic way to reduce debt.

These are the fundamental ways to begin reducing credit card debt, but what of other debts? When it comes to paying off debt it is generally far easier to do than people realize because many of the same methods apply to all debts. Paying more than the minimum reduces interest rates which saves money in the long run, as stated before. Living below one's means also saves money and reduces the risk of incurring any more debt due to having more money to set aside. Paying bills on time eliminates any late charges that may occur, which also means that no late payments appear on a credit report to affect a person's credit score. What this all boils down to is that the best way to reduce debt is to prevent unnecessary debt in the first place. Life does not work out easily enough to always be able to prevent debt, however, so the best course of action following prevention is smart management.

There is a popular idea that can not only help with debt but also improve one's credit score and it is concerning the number of credit cards a person should have. One big factor in a person's credit report is the diversification of credit. When an individual has multiple lines of credit that are in good standing then their credit limit actually increases. This is because the multiple credit cards that are well maintained tell the credit bureaus that the person is trustworthy and reliable enough to handle several lines of credit, meaning that the individual is not a risk. For example, a person with 5 credit cards in good standing is somebody that is responsible and understanding of how to manage their financial accounts according to credit bureaus. The result of this is an improvement to a person's credit score. So, what about helping with debt?

With multiple credit card accounts a person is able to have access to credit cards with different interest rates. This means that the practice of transferring account balances from high interest cards to lower interest cards is available to a person to a greater degree due to the number of credit cards they have. As stated before in this chapter, transferring accounts should only be performed when a person is able to pay off a credit card in a short amount of time. Should a person with multiple credit cards adopt this tactic then they not only improve upon their credit but they also reduce their debt.

This leads to the ultimate question; just how many credit cards should a person have in their name? The answer is that there actually is not a single universal number of credit cards a person should have. The factors that would go into determining such an answer are simply too numerous and volatile to keep track of, even creditors have trouble with the notion. The general rule of thumb is that it is ultimately up to the individual and their credit how many credit cards they should have. A person with poor credit may find that having multiple credit cards allows them to establish multiple lines of credit, which looks good on a credit report, and by consolidating the payments on the cards they in turn are able to not just reduce their debt but also increase their credit score. The inverse in of this is also true in that a person with good credit may find that having only one or two credit cards is more than adequate as they are satisfied with their credit score and they are not attempting to game the system and improve the standing.

The best course of action is to therefore take it one credit card at a time. If a person is able to make more than the monthly amount owed on a credit card, and do so consistently, then getting another credit card with lower interest rates may be the best course of action so that they can begin to improve their credit score.

Ultimately managing debt can be difficult but with proper knowledge and smart habits then debt becomes less of a hindrance and more of a way to build better credit. Debt is sometimes unavoidable and neglecting it can lead to serious damage to a person's credit score. The key is to not let debt get out of hand and to begin managing it immediately.

Some tips to keep in mind when managing debt is to always make payments that are more than minimum asked. Doing this not only pays the bill but it keeps interest rates manageable while building a positive credit score at the same time, which is the end goal of reducing debt. Also, one should remember to budget. Budgeting does not have to be an endeavor that ends with a person picking through a trash can to find items that are "still good" or spending an entire afternoon clipping coupons. Budgeting is merely keeping track of what is spent and what is owed at specified times. This also plays into living below one's means. This is a good money saving habit that goes a long way towards reducing excessive and unnecessary spending, just keep in mind that it does not have to mean that a person is living off of pre-packaged noodles. Also, there is the issue of credit cards. Credit cards should be snow balled to lower or zero interest cards whenever possible in order to reduce credit card debt incurred through interest. Doing this tactic not only builds credit over time but it saves money in the process despite the fact that the individual owns a number of credit cards to their name. Also, there is magic number or formula for figuring out just how many credit cards a person can have. It is all up to the individual and their own financial status. If they are able to handle having a large number of credit cards responsibly then they should do so.

Over all, once a person has a handle on their debt, the rest of their financial endeavors can begin to fall into place. They have learned how to read their credit report and understand the impacts of the various financial actions that they may make can have on their credit score. They also know the degree to which they can make a direct impact on their credit scores in either a positive or negative way. In other words, this is a person that is ready to make the necessary changes to their spending and understanding of money in order to begin building a more successful credit score.

Chapter 4
Credit Mistakes

When it comes to credit reports there is one thing that should be taken into consideration. What should be understood is that mistakes happen. These mistakes are not "mistakes" in the sense of some irresponsible action on the part of the consumer or anything of a similar nature. Instead these mistakes are actually errors that appear on a credit report. The erroneous information on the credit report could be reported incorrectly, belong to some other person, or even be against the law.

The fact that these errors can occur is a reason why it is important for a person to check their credit report. According to the Federal Trade Commission 25% of Americans have at least one major error in their credit reports. These errors are causing the millions of people to have worse credit than they actually have, which means that they are paying more for things that they are supposed to pay. This causes the snowball effect where they incur more debts, higher fees, and even loss of financial opportunities all through no fault of their own. In short, credit mistakes are dangerous.

In order to avoid the path of financial danger a person should carefully look over their credit report to spot errors that could actually be hurting their credit. Thankfully many of the errors are easy to spot and can be reported in order to repair the damage done. The most common credit report errors fall under three categories: personal information errors, account related errors, and derogatory mark errors.

Derogatory marks are long lasting negative records on a credit report. These marks generally last for at least 7 years on a credit report and have a huge ability to hurt a person's credit. Bankruptcy, tax liens, collections, and foreclosures are examples of derogatory marks. Because of the severity of damage derogatory marks can cause errors of this sort are especially dangerous.

There are a few key things to look for when it comes to derogatory mark errors. One such error to be wary of is a collections account that has been paid off still remaining on the credit report as unpaid. This is an obvious error that is easy to dispute. There will be documentation showing that the account has been paid and contacting the creditor directly often leads to satisfactory results in getting the issue resolved.

Another common derogatory mark error is a paid tax lien that has remained on a credit report for more than 7 years after the last date of payment. While an unpaid tax lien may stay on a credit report indefinitely, there is simply no reason for a tax lien that has been paid to remain after 7 years. It is a black mark on a credit report that does not need to exist.

A discharged account displayed as an active balance is also a key error to keep an eye on. This is perhaps the most damaging of derogatory marks because it concerns bankruptcy. A person files for bankruptcy as a last resort in order to gain some relief from debt obligations. The individual has entered into a legal process in an attempt to address overwhelming debt. Bankruptcy changes the accounts a person holds and the person no longer has the same active balances they had before filing for bankruptcy. Therefore, when a discharged account appears on a credit report as active what this does to a person's credit is damage it even further than is legally allowed. The bankrupt accounts are already in a special legal process to prevent further debts and that means it is close to impossible to actually have an active account with a balance.

These derogatory mark errors should be immediately disputed in order to prevent any further damage to one's credit. While all credit errors should be disputed, it is the derogatory marks that are the most damaging due to the sheer amount of time they remain on a credit report and the severity of the impact they can incur on an individual. A person that erroneously has an unpaid tax lien on their credit report could potentially be feeling the financial effect of that mistake for life simply because they didn't look at their credit report and dispute the mistake. The other common types of errors should not be discounted however.

Account related errors are mistakes that occur which are still damaging but not to the same severity as derogatory marks. These are errors tend to be simple fixes that take little effort to correct and probably only occur as an oversight.

An example of an account related error is a late payment that has remained on the credit report after 7 years. Generally, a credit report only lists negative information on an account for 7 years, after which it is removed from the credit report. It should be noted that the debt negative items cause still exist and still impact a person's credit. However, after the allotted time they can no longer incur more of an effect, in other words the 7-year mark is the ceiling for damage to a credit report. When a late payment remains on a credit report after this time that means it is still causing a negative impact on a person's credit. This should not appear on a credit report and should be disputed.

Another common account related error is one that is more the result of simple human error, however it could still have a negative impact if left undisputed. A loan or credit card listed on a credit report that does not belong to the individual is an error that happens on a regular basis. There could be any number of reasons for these to appear but usually it is the result of a person that had a simple mix-up while entering data. The worst-case scenario is actually a more frightening occurrence because the erroneous accounts could be the result of fraud or identity theft.

The first thing to do in either scenario is for the individual to report the false accounts directly to the credit bureau which lists the accounts. This can be done by mail, fax, email, or over the phone. It is quicker to do it by phone however disputing the account by mail provides a paper trail that can be used to support the claim that the person is actively trying to dispute the false accounts. Whichever method is chosen the following step should be to close the damaging account to prevent any future harm. Thankfully the process of fixing this error often proves successful and the fraudulent or erroneous account will be removed efficiently from the credit report.

The final category of credit mistakes is erroneous personal information. This category is the least damaging of mistakes but still has an effect on a person's credit. Like account related errors, these mistakes can often simply be attributed to human error. Thankfully personal information mistakes are the easiest to fix due to them not being directly related to financial actions.

The most common error when it comes to personal information is simply having the wrong name listed. This could be as harmless as spelling a person's name incorrectly or using an individual's maiden name after they've married. Another common error is a wrong mailing address listed on a credit report. Perhaps a person with a similar name lived at the mistaken address and whomever is responsible for correcting that information simply overlooked it. This could also happen when a person's employer information is displayed inaccurately on a credit report, a person with a similar name may have been employed by the mistaken employer.

Generally, mistakes in personal information have little to no effect on an individual's credit score. Unless the error is related to something along the lines of fraud or identity theft then there is no reason to be worried. Simply reporting to the creditors the mistake in personal information is enough to fix the problem and no harm would be done to the person's credit.

When these mistakes are made they can be removed from a person's credit report. These items are also automatically removed after the regulatory 7 years have passed, generally. However, it is also possible to remove all negative items from a credit report. The process is not difficult and can go a long way towards improving a person's credit standing.

One of the most surprising and efficient ways to remove a negative item such as a late payment is to write a letter. Often called a goodwill letter or goodwill adjustment, a person can write (or call, although writing is better) to a creditor to get a late payment forgiven and thus removed from a credit report. This tends to work best if a person has a good history with the creditor as that makes them more likely to forgive the late payment as a one-time issue.

When contacting the creditor a few key things must be discussed with them for the best results. First of all, an explanation is owed to the creditor for the late payment. Telling the creditor the financial situation that led to the payment being late could generate some understanding and sympathy. People are not perfect and unexpected events do occur, after all. Creditors are not machines but are institutions ran by people who can relate to what another person is going through.

What should also be discussed with the creditor is an explanation of the history with the creditor. A person that reminds the creditor that they have been in great standing with no issue can reinforce the fact that the late payment was not a regular occurrence. Requesting the removal of the negative mark should be made only after it has been established that there will be no repeat of late payments.

This tactic of writing the creditor to remove the late payment from a credit report is often more successful than people would imagine. Creditors are always willing to negotiate with people because they want their business. It should be noted that writing the creditor to request the removal of a late payment only works for those who are in good standing with the creditor. A person with a history of late payments is far less likely to get a sympathetic response as they have not shown that they are trust worthy. However even in that scenario it is still very likely that the creditor would be willing to negotiate a payment plan at the very least.

Regardless of the one's standing with a creditor it is always a helpful and beneficial plan to contact them. If a person is not able to remove the negative marks from their credit report then they are still going to be able to discuss options that will lead to positive impacts to a credit score in the future.

That is the biggest secret to getting negative items removed from a credit report, simply contacting the creditor. Many people are afraid of doing so because they feel that it would be difficult or they simply want to avoid the confrontation, but it cannot be stressed enough that a creditor is always willing to negotiate. Combining this with the fact that the passage of time can generally takes care of negative marks on a credit report and that leaves a clean credit report. In conjunction with a person checking their credit report for mistakes and monitoring changes results in a credit report that will remain free of negative marks for as long as the individual continues to be responsible.

Credit mistakes are common, that much is clear. With the proper tools and understanding is far easier than people realize to fix these errors, especially since these errors are not the result of negligent or poor behavior on the part of the individual but rather that of the financial institutions, creditors, and bureaus. Mistakes happen, that much is unavoidable. What should be done to fix these mistakes, regardless of who is at fault, is swift and steady action on the part of the wronged person. There is simply no reason or benefit to walking around with a debt on a person's record that should not be there. Nor is there any reason to ignore their credit report and the mistakes listed on them. Vigilance is a requirement in order to make sure one's credit standing is as accurate as possible. Bureaus and other financial institutions are run by humans, not machines, so mistakes should be expected. Again, staying vigilant is the key.

Chapter 5
Credit Boosting

There is one final aspect that requires attention when it comes to a person's credit score, and that is how to actually improve it. A number of tools and resources are available that suggest that they can improve a person's credit, but generally speaking they actually do no such thing. It is not unheard of for a person to pay a company to help improve their credit only for the company to run away with their money. Thankfully there are tested and accurate ways to quickly and permanently improve a person's credit and help ensure that they will have a happier financial future.

The first thing to do is to make sure that the credit report is accurate. The importance of this has already been discussed but as a reminder false information can hurt a credit report. Disputing the mistakes will clean up the credit report and leave a far more accurate credit score. With the knowledge of what the actual credit report is a person is then able to begin the process of improving their score. As a general rule, a person should not rely on just one credit report but should instead look at the credit reports from all of the 3 major bureaus in order to get the most accurate information possible.

The next step is to pay off any outstanding debts that are still on the credit report. The best method for doing so is to look at what is owed and choose to pay off either the debt that has the highest interest rate first or the debt that is simply the largest. The high interest rate debt is the most damaging to a person's credit and should be taken care of immediately to curb the harm it could cause. Transferring a credit card balance to a lower interest card is always a great idea to prevent the damage of high interest debt, as an example. When it comes to the debt that is the largest then the best course of action is to make payments on time, every time. In both cases, and with all debts in general, payments should be made that are more than the minimum.

Simply paying the minimum is prolonging the problem. Interest rates will continue to hurt a person's credit score and the amount owed will exist for far longer than is necessary. If a person cannot pay more than the minimum amount then contacting the creditor directly can reveal options that can make it easier on the individual. Creditors are always willing to negotiate and there is no harm making a deal that could alleviate debt or debt payment issues.

Aside from debt management there are other ways to significantly boost a credit score. One such method is in regard to the FICO score. Because a large portion of the FICO score is based on a ratio of credit used versus credit available, a proven way to increase a person's score is to game this ratio.

Gaming the FICO score is actually very simple and can be seen as a criticism of credit scores in the United States, however this can be exploited to the benefit of people looking to improve their score. One of the more common ways to improve this score is to simply get an increase on the credit limit of a credit card.

The increase in the credit limit automatically improves the utilization ratio of credit used versus credit available. As an example, if a credit card has a $200 limit but $100 is utilized then that is a 50% ratio. However, if the limit is $1000 while the utilization remains at $100 then the ratio becomes 10%, which significantly improves a credit score as it shows that the individual is less of a financial risk. There are two important facets of this to keep in mind that could potentially have a negative effect on a person's credit.

First of all, only one credit card should get an increased limit otherwise the individual looks too risky to creditors. Pick a single credit card and only increase the credit line on that one. The second factor to consider is that requesting an increase often results in what is called a hard pull. A hard pull is a thorough evaluation of one's credit report by a lender and they cause a negative, albeit small, impact on a credit score. A hard pull remains on a credit report for 2 years and multiple hard pulls can add up to hurting a credit score. This is also why it is important to only use one credit card to increase the limit of it so that the individual does not incur unnecessary credit damage for making multiple requests.

Another way to improve a credit score also takes advantage of credit utilization. When it comes to credit card payments. making large lump sum payments quickly reduces the utilization ratio.

Combining this with the increased credit limit often results in a significant jump in a person's credit score. It should be noted that when using this method, it is not the dollar amounts that is important but the rather the ratio that is key. There is no difference between paying $5 for a $10 limit with $2 utilization and paying $500 for a $1000 limit with $200 utilization when it comes to the ratio.

Opening a secured credit card is a safe method of improving a credit score. A secured credit card is different from a normal credit card in that it functions similar to a checking account in that a person deposits money into it. What this does is "secure" the line of credit and shows creditors that the individual is trustworthy enough to handle a line of credit. This is best for those with bad credit and those who are just starting to build credit, however the benefits to the credit score make it useful to everybody regardless of their credit situation.

One more method is available for boosting one's credit score, however it should be noted its viability is dependent on the person's current credit standing. Refinancing is an often used financial option that can lead to lower monthly payments as well as lower interest rates. What refinancing means is paying off old loans with new loans. This is a common tactic people use when they want to lower their monthly payments or get better interest rates, in much a similar fashion as transferring a credit balance.

Refinancing causes the old loan to be closed and some bureaus may still factor that in that loan when looking at the age of the accounts. This could be a negative impact to those who have had a loan for an extended amount of time as a result. There is a tradeoff that can offset this impact for those with younger accounts. The new loans will be added to the total number of accounts associated with a person's credit report and that could help increase their credit score.

Ultimately refinancing is not as viable for those with old loans and accounts, but it could be a boon for others who have newer accounts and loans. This is why the viability of refinancing rests on the individual's credit score, the ability to improve the credit score depends on if the person has old loans or new loans.

With all of the factors taken into consideration a person is able to greatly increase their credit score in a short amount of time. Increasing the credit limit improves without increasing spending improves the credit ratio greatly, which further goes to increase the credit score. Paying off debts with large payments rather than just the minimum also serves the purpose of increasing the credit score. Of course, no action should be taken without first taking into account what is actually on an individual's credit report.

Conclusion

Thank you for making it through to the end of *Credit Score: How to Remove all Negative Items from Your Credit Report and Boost Your Credit Score by 100 Points in 30 Days or Less*, hopefully it was informative enough and able to provide you with all of the tools needed to begin your journey towards a better credit score.

The next step in the process is to begin to put what you have learned to practice. Begin by requesting free credit reports and free credit scores from all of the available bureaus. Any errors found in those credit reports should be immediately disputed so that you are no longer hurting your credit score with negative items. Following that you should then be prepared to create a budget that will reinforce your new financial plan that is designed to increase your credit score. It is not too difficult and you should be able to eliminate your unnecessary debts in the process.

Do not be afraid to live below your means if you have to. It is a healthy tactic that can not only save money in the long run but may also expose you to a kind of life that is better suited to your tastes. Also, do not forget to overlook the obvious. If a late payment is leaving a black mark on your credit report then there is no reason to dismiss the idea of simply mailing a letter, or making a phone call, to explain what happened. Remind them of your history with them and that your late payment was a one-time thing and you'll find that your record may have the late payment removed.

This is perhaps one of the biggest lessons to take away from this book: be vigilant towards your credit report. There are a number of resources available and they are all viable. A bureau, a lender, a bank, and other financial institutions are all ran by people and people are prone to mistakes. It has been stated before but it will be stated again for emphasis, do not let errors found on the credit go ignored. The damage they could cause should be eliminated as soon as possible. Lastly, be sure to tackle either the biggest debt first or the item that has the largest interest rate first.

At that point, you will be ready to boost your credit score and reap the rewards that come with having healthy credit. The negative impacts of your previous credit score will disappear and you will be able to enjoy the financial status that you deserve. Loan approvals will become much more easily obtained, job opportunities will improve, and potential homes will be available for rent or purchase that otherwise would be been out of reach.

One last thing, if you found this book useful in anyway then please leave a review on Amazon. It would be greatly appreciated!

www.ingramcontent.com/pod-product-compliance
Lightning Source LLC
Chambersburg PA
CBHW050026230526
45470CB00003B/1145